Traveling Butterflies

Susumu Shingu

Owlkids Books

One day in the short summer of a country up north,

a tiny creature wakes up inside
an egg as small as a dewdrop.

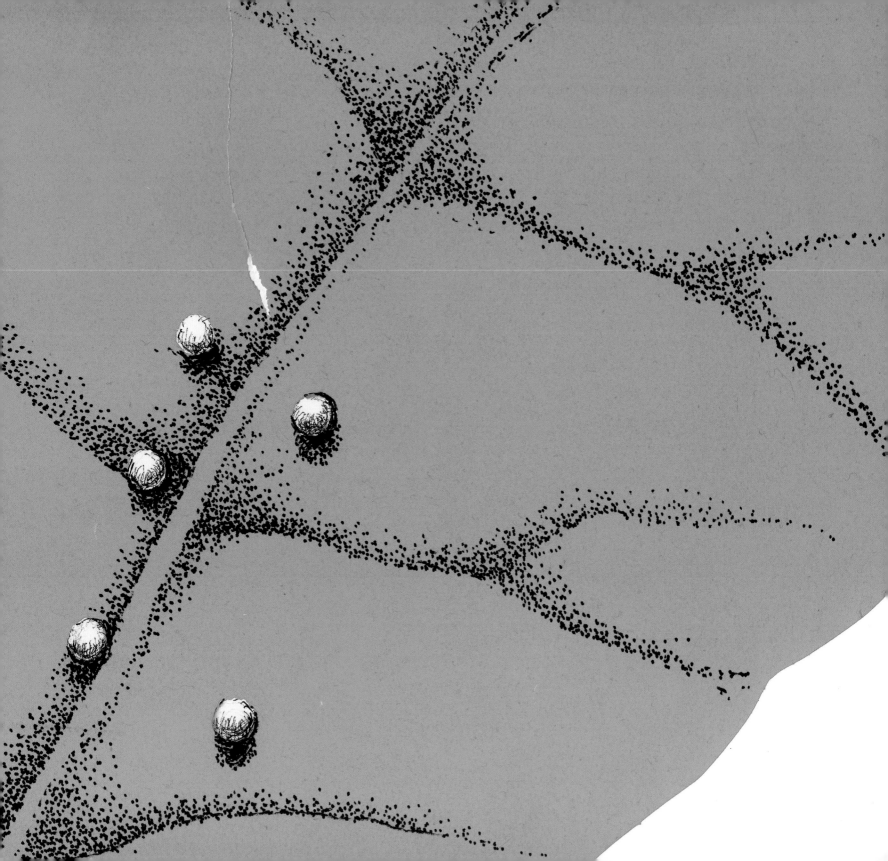

She eats to grow bigger and bigger, munching on lots of milkweed.

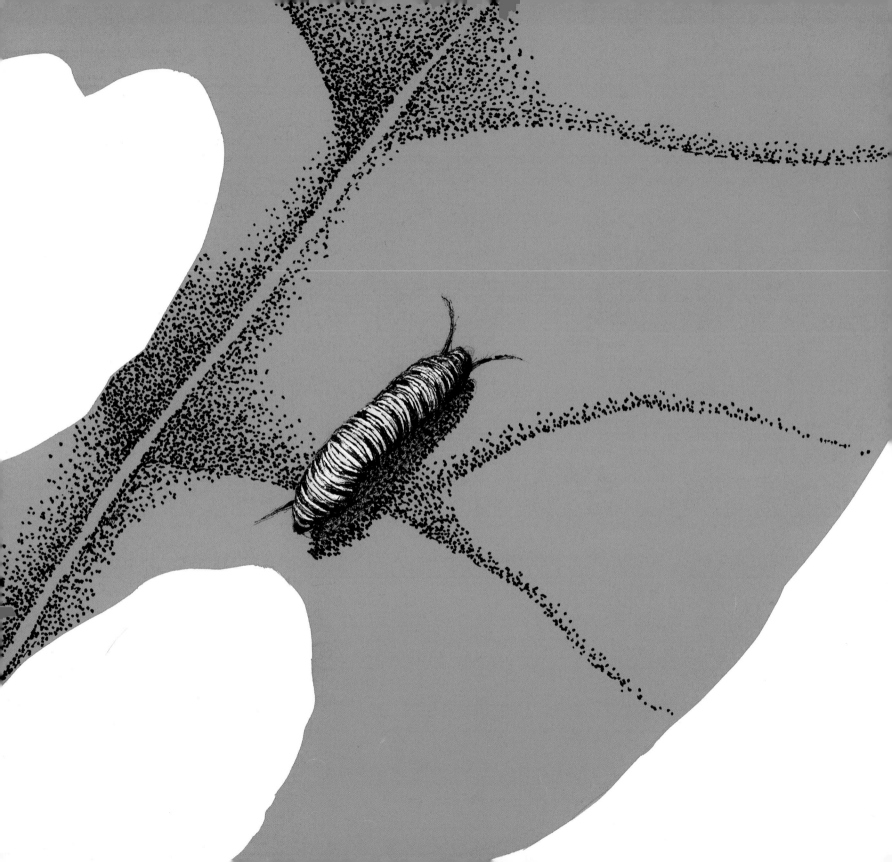

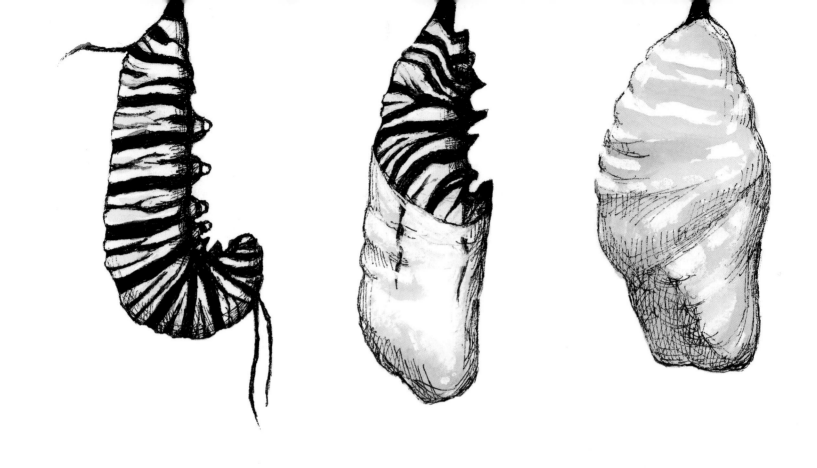

When she's big enough, she wraps a
cocoon around herself like a veil.

When she breaks out, she has changed!

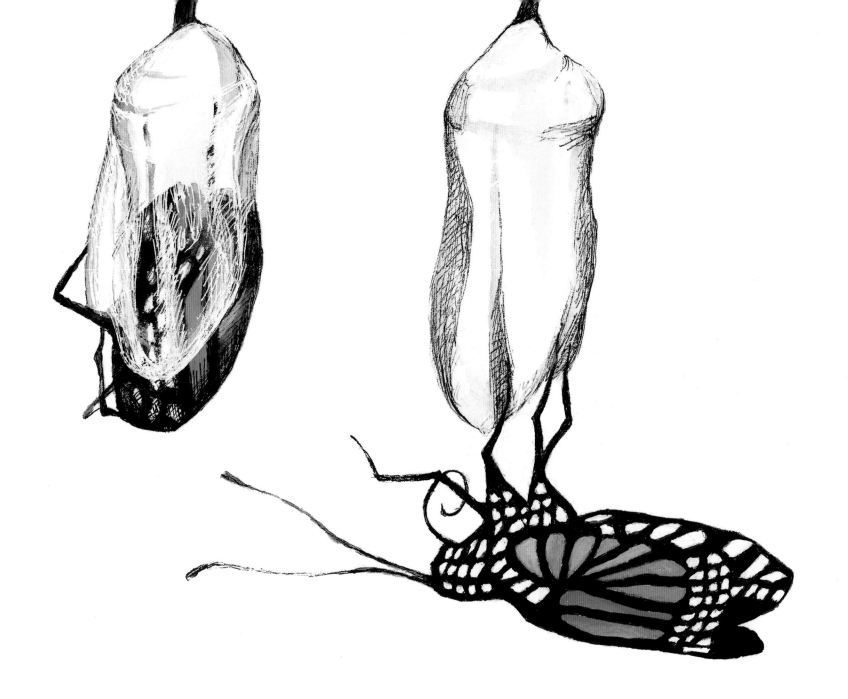

Her new wings look
like stained glass.

Now she needs to drink lots of
sweet nectar for her long journey.

She knows when it's time to take off,
riding the southward wind,

sailing over an enormous lake,

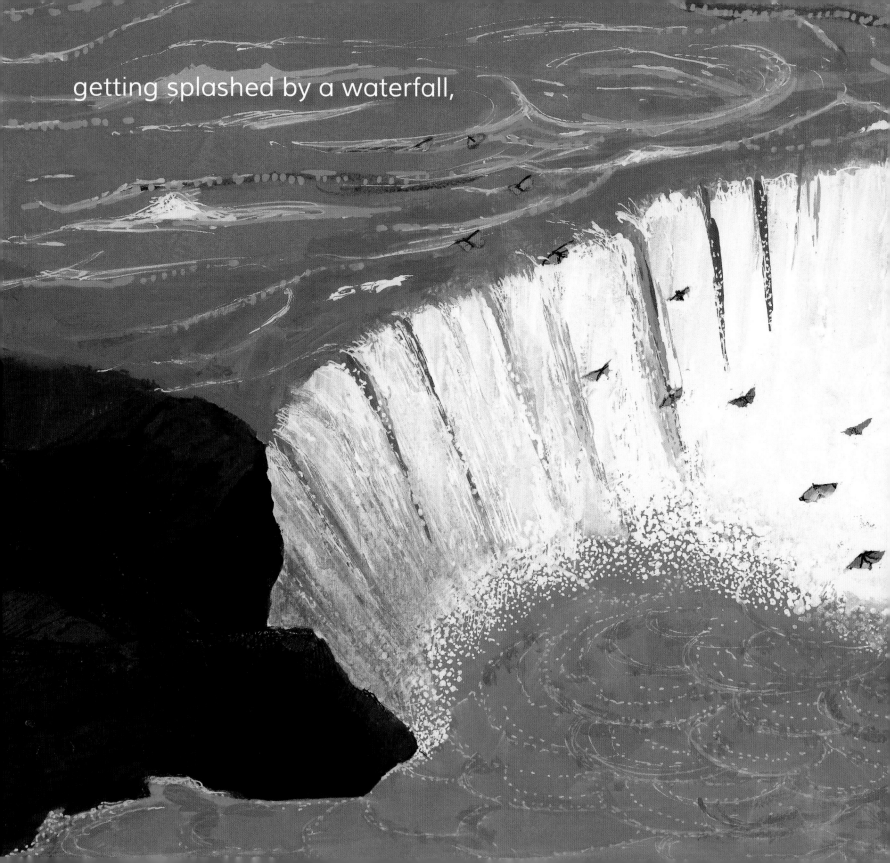

getting splashed by a waterfall,

busily flying over big cities,

and resting under leaves on rainy days.

She visits villages

and crosses over rivers and plains.

The southern forest is getting closer and closer.

The trees
are turning
a deeper and
deeper orange.

The forest is an ideal place
for butterflies to mate.

Huddling close, they slumber in peace,

so they can take off again

to travel back to the north country.

More about monarch butterflies

The monarch butterfly is a small species weighing around 0.02 ounces (0.6 grams) with a wingspan of about 4 inches (10 centimeters). These tiny creatures migrate great distances every year. Scientists have studied their migration routes by marking their wings and collecting reports of sightings. In the 1970s, the monarchs' winter sanctuary was discovered in the mountains of Mexico.

Most butterflies live short lives of only two to six weeks. But mysteriously, the generation of monarchs that migrates south lives a surprising six to eight months. They start flying south from Canada and the northernmost parts of the United States at summer's end and reach the Mexican forest after two months of flying, covering nearly 2,500 miles (4,000 kilometers).

After spending the winter in Mexico, the monarchs begin the return trip north in the spring. The butterflies born in the south live the usual two to six weeks. This means that it can take three to four generations of monarchs to make the trip back to their northern home. Researchers aren't sure how new generations of monarchs know to fly the same route and find the same forest every year. There's still so much to learn about these traveling butterflies.

Published in North America in 2015 by Owlkids Books Inc.

First published in Japan in 2012 by EDUCATIONAL FOUNDATION BUNKA GAKUEN BUNKA PUBLISHING BUREAU (Sunao Onuma, publisher), Tokyo

English translation rights arranged with EDUCATIONAL FOUNDATION BUNKA GAKUEN BUNKA PUBLISHING BUREAU through Japan Foreign-Rights Centre

Owlkids Books acknowledges the financial support of the Canada Council for the Arts, the Ontario Arts Council, the Government of Canada through the Canada Book Fund (CBF) and the Government of Ontario through the Ontario Media Development Corporation's Book Initiative for our publishing activities.

Published in Canada by
Owlkids Books Inc.
10 Lower Spadina Avenue
Toronto, ON M5V 2Z2

Published in the United States by
Owlkids Books Inc.
1700 Fourth Street
Berkeley, CA 94710

Library and Archives Canada Cataloguing in Publication

Shingū, Susumu, 1937- [Tabisuru chō. English]
     Traveling butterflies / Susumu Shingu.

Translation of: Tabisuru chō.

ISBN 978-1-77147-148-0 (bound)

    1. Monarch butterfly--Juvenile literature. 2. Monarch butterfly-- Migration--Juvenile literature. I. Title. III. Title: Tabisuru chō. English

QL561.D3S5513 2015   595.78'9   C2014-908050-6

Library of Congress Control Number: 2014958762

Manufactured in Dongguan, China, in March 2015, by Toppan Leefung Packaging & Printing (Dongguan) Co., Ltd.
Job #BAYDC15

A   B   C   D   E   F

Publisher of Chirp, chickaDEE and OWL
www.owlkidsbooks.com